# THE CIVIL RIGHTS MOVEMENT THROUGH THE EYES OF LYNDON B. JOHNSON

by Moira Rose Donohue

**Content Consultant**
Françoise N. Hamlin
Departments of Africana Studies & History
Brown University

**Core Library**
An Imprint of Abdo Publishing
abdopublishing.com

**abdopublishing.com**

Published by Abdo Publishing, a division of ABDO, PO Box 398166, Minneapolis, Minnesota 55439. Copyright © 2016 by Abdo Consulting Group, Inc. International copyrights reserved in all countries. No part of this book may be reproduced in any form without written permission from the publisher. Core Library™ is a trademark and logo of Abdo Publishing.

Printed in the United States of America, North Mankato, Minnesota
092015
012016

**THIS BOOK CONTAINS RECYCLED MATERIALS**

Cover Photo: AP Images
Interior Photos: AP Images, 1, 19, 20, 24, 35, 45; Bettmann/Corbis, 4, 22, 28, 31, 36, 38; Keystone Pictures USA/ZumaPress/Newscom, 6; Schulman-Sachs/Picture-Alliance/Newscom, 9; Bill Hudson/AP Images, 12; William J. Smith/AP Images, 15; Red Line Editorial, 18, 26; Charles Knoblock/AP Images, 32

Editor: Jon Westmark
Series Designer: Laura Polzin

**Library of Congress Control Number: 2015945401**

**Cataloging-in-Publication Data**
Donohue, Moira Rose.
 The Civil Rights Movement through the eyes of Lyndon B. Johnson / Moira Rose Donohue.
  p. cm. -- (Presidential perspectives)
ISBN 978-1-68078-029-1 (lib. bdg.)
Includes bibliographical references and index.
1. Civil rights movements--United States--Juvenile literature.  2. Johnson, Lyndon B. (Lyndon Baines), 1908-1973--Juvenile literature.  3. Presidents--United States--Juvenile literature.  I. Title.
973.923--dc23

                                                      2015945401

# CONTENTS

# CHAPTER ONE

# AN IMPOSSIBLE TIME

President Lyndon B. Johnson picked up the phone. It was late on November 25, 1963. It had been a hard day. But he needed to make one more call. At 9:40 p.m., Dr. Martin Luther King Jr. answered the president's call. King was a leader of the civil rights movement. The movement worked to establish equal treatment for African Americans. King thanked the president for his interest in civil rights. He told

Lyndon B. Johnson took office on November 22, 1963. He felt it was important to reach out to civil rights leaders, such as King, early during his time in office.

Johnson took the oath of presidential office just hours after Kennedy was killed.

Johnson he knew it was a difficult time for the US government.

"It's just an impossible period," Johnson responded.

Just days before, on November 22, 1963, there was a different president of the United States. President John F. Kennedy was visiting Dallas, Texas, when he was shot and killed in his car on the way to an event. Johnson was Kennedy's vice president. He was riding in a car behind Kennedy's at the time of the shooting.

The afternoon of Kennedy's death, Johnson was sworn in as president on the president's plane, Air Force One. He addressed the nation from the airport in Washington, DC. "This is a sad time for all people," he said. "For me it is a deep, personal tragedy."

## Still Not Equal

Johnson grew up in Texas. Over the years, he traveled throughout the South, which was legally segregated at the time. Segregation laws forced African Americans to use facilities separate from white Americans. The facilities were often in poor condition. Johnson witnessed the humiliation African Americans felt when they were forced to use these facilities. Like Kennedy, Johnson believed in equality for all Americans, regardless of race. He saw many people around the country pushing for change.

While talking to King, Johnson listed several bills he wanted Congress to pass. One was a civil

## Letter from Birmingham Jail

In 1954 the Supreme Court said public schools must be integrated. But the ruling did not apply to other public places. For example, African Americans could not use the same buses, restaurants, or swimming pools as white Americans. Civil rights groups planned peaceful protests to make people aware African Americans were not being treated fairly. Some groups intentionally disobeyed the segregation laws. In April 1963, King led demonstrations in Birmingham, Alabama. He was sent to jail for his actions. From jail he wrote a strong letter against segregation. It helped draw attention to the unfair treatment of African Americans.

rights bill. In June 1963, Kennedy had asked a member of Congress to introduce the bill. Days before his death, Kennedy urged Congress to consider it.

"We've got to not give up on any of them," Johnson told King.

King said it would be a tribute to Kennedy if Congress passed the civil rights bill.

## In His Memory

One part of Kennedy's civil rights bill would allow African Americans to use the same public places, such as hotels

Johnson urged Congress to pass Kennedy's civil rights bill.

and restaurants, as white Americans. Kennedy sent the bill to Congress on June 22, 1963. It went to the Rules Committee of the House of Representatives. The Rules Committee decides the order in which bills get discussed. It also decides how long a bill can be discussed before it is voted on.

The Rules Committee refused to make any decisions about the civil rights bill. The head of the committee, Representative Howard Smith of Virginia,

## March on Washington

In the spring of 1963, civil rights leaders began planning a demonstration in Washington, DC. Their goal was to bring an end to segregation laws. Kennedy hoped the event's organizers would postpone the march until his bill went through Congress. On June 22, he met with the event organizers. During the meeting, Kennedy agreed to support the rally. In return the civil rights leaders agreed not to speak against the bill at the event. On August 28, 1963, more than 250,000 people gathered peacefully in Washington, DC. They sang songs and heard speeches. King ended the day with his famous "I Have a Dream" speech.

wanted to block the bill from being debated by the House.

On November 27, 1963, Johnson stood before Congress. It was only five days after Kennedy's death and two days since his conversation with King. Johnson knew he was about to give the most important speech of his life. He urged Congress to pass the bill. Echoing King, Johnson said it was the best way to honor President Kennedy's memory.

Kennedy gave a speech to the nation on June 11, 1963, about the need for a civil rights law. In his speech, he used the word *Negro* to refer to African Americans, a common practice in the 1960s. The following is part of Kennedy's speech:

> It ought to be possible, in short, for every American to enjoy the privileges of being American without regard to his race or his color. . . . But this is not the case today.
>
> The Negro baby born in America today, regardless of the section of the nation in which he is born, has about one-half as much chance of completing high school as a white baby born in the same place on the same day, one-third as much chance of completing college, one-third as much chance of becoming a professional man, twice as much chance of becoming unemployed, about one-seventh as much chance of earning $10,000 a year, a life expectancy which is seven years shorter, and the prospects of earning only half as much.

Source: John F. Kennedy. "Report to the American People on Civil Rights." John F. Kennedy Presidential Library and Museum. n.p., June 11, 1963. Web. Accessed April 14, 2015.

## Back It Up

Kennedy uses evidence to support his point of view. Write a paragraph in your own words describing his main point. Then write two or three facts Kennedy uses to make this point.

# CHAPTER TWO

# THIS CANNOT CONTINUE

On New Year's Eve in 1963, a little more than a month after his call with King, Johnson went to a party. It was held at the Faculty Club at the University of Texas. He strolled in with his new personal secretary, Gerri Whittington. Whittington was African American. The club was segregated. Johnson's actions sent Congress and the country a message: he supported civil rights protesters around the country.

A 17-year-old civil rights protester is attacked by a police dog in Birmingham, Alabama, on May 3, 1963.

## Struggle for Change

In the spring of 1963, activists in Birmingham, Alabama, started a new campaign for African-American rights. The Birmingham Campaign consisted of months of peaceful protests. Police in Birmingham responded with violence, using dogs and fire hoses against African Americans. It helped convince Kennedy to introduce the civil rights bill to Congress. The protests helped change local laws. But some white Americans were upset about the changing laws. On September 15, 1963, segregationists bombed an African-American church in Birmingham, killing four African-American girls.

He would join the fight to end segregation.

Congress heard the message. On January 30, 1964, the House Rules Committee sent Kennedy's civil rights bill forward. At noon on January 31, 1964, the House of Representatives began debating the bill.

Many representatives from southern states objected to the bill. They argued it took power away from state governments. Some members of the House offered amendments, or changes, to the bill.

Virginia representative Howard Smith, *left*, attempted to block many civil rights bills as chairman of the Rules Committee.

Representative Howard Smith added an amendment to end job discrimination against women. Many people think Smith hoped this amendment would turn some members against the bill. But it did not work out that way. On February 10, 1964, the House passed the bill with Smith's amendment. The vote was 290–130.

## The Filibuster

Next the bill went to the Senate for approval. Johnson knew the bill would face a bigger battle

## Stealing the Floor

The word *filibuster* comes from a Dutch word meaning "pirate." A filibuster allows senators to "steal" the floor to prevent a vote. At the time of the debate about the civil rights bill, the filibuster rules allowed senators to talk about any topic. Sometimes they read from books. The only way to end the filibuster was with a vote of cloture. At the time, cloture required a two-thirds majority vote. Today only 60 votes are needed.

there. Debates are done differently in the Senate. There is no Rules Committee to say how long the Senate can discuss a bill. Senators can drag out a debate by filibustering. A filibuster is when a senator or group of senators talks for a very long time in order to prevent a vote on a bill. At the time, only a two-thirds majority vote by the Senate could end a filibuster. This meant the Senate needed 67 votes to pass the bill instead of a normal majority of 51 votes.

In March 1964, senators began a filibuster on the civil rights bill. Outside the Senate hall, Johnson worked to change senators' minds about the bill.

Johnson had been in Congress for more than 20 years. He knew it was important to work with Congress. And he had many friends there.

Johnson asked Clarence Mitchell Jr. for help. Mitchell worked for a civil rights organization called the National Association for the Advancement of Colored People (NAACP). He spoke with senators as well.

Johnson, Mitchell, and others changed senators' minds one by one. Finally they thought they had at least 67 senators to vote to end the filibuster. On June 10, 1964, the clerk took the vote. The vote was 71–29. It was more than enough to end the filibuster. The 75-day filibuster, the longest in the history of the Senate, was over.

## Seventy-five Pens

Civil rights protestors continued to draw national attention to civil rights issues. On June 11, 1964, King and others protested segregation laws in Saint Augustine, Florida. The group of African Americans

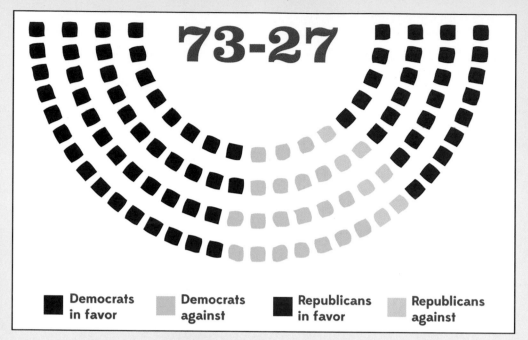

**73-27**

| Democrats in favor | Democrats against | Republicans in favor | Republicans against |

**The Senate Vote**

This chart shows how the 100 members of the Senate voted on the Civil Rights Act of 1964. How does the vote compare to the vote to end the filibuster? What do you notice about how each political party voted?

attempted to eat at a segregated restaurant. King and the other protestors were arrested and sent to jail. Many other protests like this continued around the country.

On June 19, 1964, the Senate passed the civil rights bill. It outlawed segregation in public places. It also promised equal employment for all races and for

Johnson signs the Civil Rights Act on July 2, 1964.

women. The bill became known as the Civil Rights Act of 1964.

On July 2, 1964, the bill went to the president. Speaking about racial discrimination, Johnson said, "It cannot continue." Using 75 different pens, Johnson signed the bill into law. He handed pens to the people who had worked hard to get the bill passed, including King and other civil rights leaders.

# IF YOU CAN'T VOTE, YOU DON'T COUNT

On Tuesday morning, March 9, 1965, President Johnson stared out a window of the White House. Hundreds of angry people gathered outside. They chanted to protest the violence African Americans were facing across the country. Two days earlier, people tried to march peacefully from Selma, Alabama, to Montgomery, the state's capital. The purpose of the march was to bring attention to the

State troopers attack voter-rights marchers in Selma, Alabama, on March 7, 1965.

An African-American man attempts to register to vote at a facility in Georgia on March 2, 1960.

fact that African Americans were being denied the right to vote. State police stopped the marchers and beat them. They sprayed the marchers with tear gas. Americans watched the event on television. Reporters called it "Bloody Sunday."

Earlier in 1965, there was another televised incident in Alabama. African-American teachers tried to register to vote, but the police blocked their way. A sheriff hit an elderly woman.

Less than a year before, Johnson signed the Civil Rights Act of 1964. Cities across the South began to follow the laws. Johnson also hired African Americans in high positions in the government. Yet racism was still causing big problems across the country.

King insisted more must be done to support civil rights. On December 18, 1964, he and Johnson spoke about voting laws. African Americans had gained the right to vote

## Top Lawyer

Part of the president's job is to appoint other people to important positions. One of the job appointments Johnson made was the solicitor general. This is the top lawyer for the United States. He or she brings cases to the Supreme Court. In 1965 Johnson asked an African American named Thurgood Marshall to take the job. Marshall had been the lead lawyer with the NAACP for many years. Johnson told Marshall he wanted people to see an African American appearing before the Supreme Court on the side of the United States. Johnson would later appoint Marshall as a Supreme Court justice.

People gather in front of the White House on March 9, 1965, to protest violence against African Americans in Alabama.

in 1870 through the Fifteenth Amendment to the US Constitution. But white Americans in the South were not allowing African Americans to register. Johnson wanted everyone to be able to vote, but he did not agree that the law needed to be changed. He told King to let courts fix the issue.

Johnson had other issues to deal with. Just days earlier, he had sent many US soldiers to Vietnam, a country in Asia. A war was taking place in the country, and fighting was getting worse.

## An American Problem

Looking out at the protest, Johnson wondered if King was right after all. He could not ignore the facts. Discrimination was still an issue for African Americans. It was a problem across the country, from the North to the South. Johnson called it "an American problem."

On March 15, 1965, Johnson spoke to Congress. He described why African Americans could not register to vote. Often white registrars told them it was too late in

## PERSPECTIVES
### Vernon Dahmer

African-American civil rights leader Vernon Dahmer liked to say, "If you can't vote, you don't count." For many years, he tried to vote in Mississippi. But his county clerk, Luther M. Cox, often made it impossible for African Americans to register. Cox and other registrars asked voters questions to make sure they could read. But if the voter was African-American, the clerks often asked difficult or impossible questions, such as "How many bubbles are in a bar of soap?" On January 6, 1966, Dahmer organized a voting registration drive in his hometown. The next day, a group of men set fire to Dahmer's home. They were upset about the registration drive. Dahmer died from his injuries.

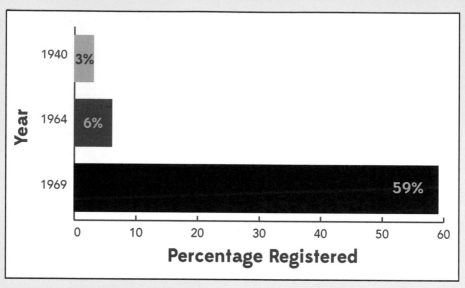

**Voting in the South**
This graph shows the percentage of voter-age African Americans registered to vote in 1940, 1964, and 1969 in the South. By what percentage did the number of southern African-American voters change from 1964 to 1969?

the day. Sometimes African Americans were told the right clerk was not on site to help them. Unlike white Americans, some registrars asked African Americans to recite the entire US Constitution from memory in order to register. Johnson asked Congress to pass a law to end this unfair treatment. After he finished his speech, Johnson's wife noted he seemed much happier. He knew he had done the right thing.

## The Voting Rights Act

Now Johnson had to convince members of Congress to support a voting rights bill. The bill passed quickly. Congress reacted to pressure from the American people. On August 6, 1965, Johnson signed the Voting Rights Act. It prevented local governments from standing in the way of African Americans registering to vote. When local registrars did not let African Americans register, the US government took over registration. At last, African Americans could choose who represented them.

## EXPLORE ONLINE

### The Constitution Says . . .

Chapter Three discusses voting rights. Read the Fifteenth Amendment of the US Constitution on the website below. How does the amendment change the way you think about what was happening to African-American voters in the South?

### Fifteenth Amendment

mycorelibrary.com/lyndon-b.-johnson

# THERE'S NO PLACE LIKE HOME

On August 11, 1965, police violence toward an African-American man sparked anger in Los Angeles, California. Riots erupted in an African-American neighborhood known as Watts. Johnson was heartbroken. It was less than a week after he signed the Voting Rights Act.

King was upset too. He and the president again spoke on the phone. Johnson asked King what more

Heavily armed National Guard troops gather in the Watts neighborhood of Los Angeles, California, on August 17, 1965.

## The City of Watts

Watts is a neighborhood in the southern part of Los Angeles, California. The area was named for Charles Watts, who owned much of the land there. It became part of Los Angeles in 1926. Large apartment buildings were constructed in Watts during World War II (1939–1945). At the time, many people worked in local manufacturing plants. After the war, manufacturing jobs became limited. Many white Americans left Watts. Unfair housing practices limited where African Americans could live. By the 1960s, Watts apartments were filled with poor African Americans. Riots broke out in 1965. They were in response to unfair policing of the area, as well as the poor quality of public schools and hospitals.

they could do to end the violence. King talked about fighting poverty.

Johnson had come from a poor family. But he was able to go to college and find good jobs. Years of discrimination made it hard for many African Americans to do the same.

Johnson and other leaders knew poverty and civil rights were linked. To fight poverty, Johnson convinced Congress to pass the Economic Opportunity Act of 1964. He wanted to help poor people in both the South

Johnson signs into law the Economic Opportunity Act of 1964, also known as the War on Poverty Bill.

and the North. The new law would help people get jobs. It was part of Johnson's plan for a "Great Society." But the law did not do enough to help people living in poor conditions. More was needed.

Johnson believed a fair housing law would help. African Americans were discriminated against when they tried to rent or buy homes. Johnson knew they

Protestors in Chicago march on August 24, 1966, to push for open housing laws. Some residents put sprinklers out to discourage the marchers.

should have the same choices as white Americans. He wanted neighborhoods to become racially mixed.

## Pushing for Change

In 1966 King called for housing law changes in Chicago. Johnson then pushed Congress to pass a bill that would give African Americans the same rights to housing as white Americans. But not all white Americans agreed with integrating neighborhoods.

And many people who rented and sold houses were opposed to the idea.

The Senate did not want the law. Johnson and King were also at odds. King spoke against Johnson for fighting the Vietnam War. King felt the United States should not be in Vietnam. He wanted the money to be spent in the United States on poverty issues. This time the bill died. The war in Vietnam took most of Johnson's time from the summer of 1964 until the end of his time as president. But he continued to ask Congress to pass an equal-housing law.

In 1968 the House passed a bill to protect civil rights workers. The Senate added an amendment. It would stop people from being able to discriminate against African Americans when renting and selling homes.

But once again, senators from the South filibustered. Votes to close the debate failed three times. Edward W. Brooke was the only African-American senator. He represented

### Senator Brooke on Housing

Senator Edward W. Brooke was born in Washington, DC. He fought for his country in World War II. During his service, the army did not allow him to use the store or swimming pool on the army base. The army said these facilities were for white soldiers only. "We were treated as second-class soldiers," Brooke said. When he returned home from the war, he could not buy the home he wanted for his family because of his race. Brooke went to law school at Boston University and became a lawyer. In 1966 he was elected as the senator of Massachusetts.

Massachusetts. Brooke and Minnesota senator Walter Mondale tried to get votes to end the debate. On March 4, Mondale told the president they needed only one more vote. President Johnson called Alaskan Senator Bob Bartlett. The senator promised to vote to end the filibuster. He did, and the Senate passed the bill. But because of the housing amendment, it was different from the bill the House originally passed. It needed to go back to the House

Senator Brooke was the first African-American US Senator to be elected by popular vote.

to be voted on again. Once again the House Rules Committee delayed the debate. It was finally set for April 9, 1968.

## From Tragedy to Triumph

Before the debate could start, tragedy struck the civil rights movement. On April 4, 1968, less than five years after Kennedy's death, King was shot and killed in Memphis, Tennessee.

More than 50,000 people gathered in Atlanta, Georgia, on April 9, 1968, to follow King's casket at a memorial service.

Johnson sent a message to Congress. He begged lawmakers to help heal the nation by passing an equal-housing law in honor of King. He spoke to individual representatives. He urged them to vote for the bill. The day of King's funeral, the House Rules Committee sent the bill to the House for debate. The next day, the House passed the Fair Housing Act and sent it to the president. On April 11, 1968, Johnson signed the bill into law.

## FURTHER EVIDENCE

Chapter Four talks about Johnson's work to get equal-housing laws passed. What is one main point of the chapter? What evidence supports it? The website at the link below is the speech Johnson made to the country after King was killed. Find a quote in his speech that supports the main point of this chapter.

### A Day of Mourning
mycorelibrary.com/lyndon-b.-johnson

# CHAPTER FIVE

# JOHNSON LEAVES OFFICE

Johnson decided in March 1968 not to run for another term as president. As he left the White House in January 1969, he talked about his accomplishments. He told reporters he was happiest about getting the Voting Rights Act passed.

Four years later, on January 22, 1973, Johnson died from a heart attack. But the civil rights laws he steered through Congress continued to have a big

Johnson, right, speaks with Richard Nixon. Nixon took over as president in January 1969.

impact on the country. Public segregation mostly ended. Federal laws protected African Americans' right to vote.

## Johnson's Legacy

Today African Americans attend the same high schools and colleges as white Americans. And African Americans have served in almost all elected positions.

Johnson did not get to see all the good that came from the laws he signed into effect. And not all the dreams he shared with civil rights workers have been realized today. But Johnson's actions made a difference. They also opened the door for equal rights for women, people with disabilities, and gay people.

After leaving office, Johnson said he was happiest about getting the Voting Rights Act passed. The following is an excerpt from Johnson's speech to Congress urging it to pass the act:

> In our time we have come to live with moments of great crisis. . . . But rarely in any time does an issue lay bare the secret heart of America itself. Rarely are we met with a challenge, not to our growth or abundance, our welfare or our security, but rather to the values and the purposes and the meaning of our beloved Nation.
>
> The issue of equal rights for American Negroes is such an issue. And should we defeat every enemy, should we double our wealth and conquer the stars, and still be unequal to this issue, then we will have failed as a people and as a nation.
>
> Source: Lyndon B. Johnson. "The American Promise." LBJ Presidential Library. Lyndon Baines Johnson Foundation, n.d. Web. August 25, 2015.

## What's the Big Idea?

Read the excerpt carefully. How are civil rights issues distinguished from other US issues? According to Johnson, in what way would Congress have failed by not passing the Voting Rights Act?

# IMPORTANT DATES

**April 16, 1963**

Martin Luther King Jr. writes his letter from jail in Birmingham, Alabama.

**June 22, 1963**

President John F. Kennedy sends civil rights bill to Congress.

**Aug. 28, 1963**

More than 250,000 people gather in Washington, DC, to protest segregation laws.

**Mar. 7, 1965**

Police attack marchers on their way from Selma to Montgomery, Alabama.

**Aug. 6, 1965**

Johnson signs the Voting Rights Act.

**Aug. 11, 1965**

Race riots start in the Watts neighborhood of Los Angeles, California.

**Nov. 22, 1963**

Kennedy dies after being shot; Lyndon B. Johnson becomes president.

**June 10, 1964**

The Senate ends its filibuster of the civil rights bill.

**July 2, 1964**

Johnson signs the Civil Rights Act of 1964.

**April 4, 1968**

King dies from a gunshot wound.

**April 11, 1968**

Johnson signs the Fair Housing Act of 1968.

**Jan. 22, 1973**

Johnson dies four years after leaving office.

## You Are There

Chapter Three talks about African Americans who tried to register to vote and were not allowed. Imagine you want to vote in a school election and are told you cannot because of your race. How would you feel? What would you do?

## Take a Stand

Lyndon B. Johnson believed education was important. He worked to earn enough money to go to college and become a teacher. As president he tried to find ways to allow African Americans to go to college. How important do you think it is to have a college education? Why?

## Surprise Me

This book talks about the ways African Americans were denied their civil rights. List several activities they were not allowed to do. Which of these surprised you the most? Why?

## Tell the Tale

Chapter Three of this book talks about the march from Selma to Montgomery, Alabama. The two cities are 53 miles (85 km) apart—a long walk. Imagine you were on the march. Write 200 words about your experiences. What did you see? Who did you meet?

# GLOSSARY

**activist**
a person who campaigns for social change

**amendment**
a change to a proposed or existing law

**bill**
a proposed law that has been introduced in Congress

**cloture**
ending or limiting debate

**debate**
to discuss or argue

**discriminate**
to treat unfairly or differently

**majority**
the larger number, usually more than half

**poverty**
the lack of money and resources to meet basic needs

**register**
to be put on a list

**segregate**
to separate people, usually according to race, sexual orientation, gender, or religious beliefs

# LEARN MORE

## Books

Gold, Susan Dudley. *Presidents and Their Times: Lyndon B. Johnson*. Tarrytown, NY: Marshall Cavendish Benchmark, 2009.

Rice, Dona Herweck. *Martin Luther King Jr.* New York: TIME for Kids, 2011.

Uhl, Xina M. *The Passing of the Civil Rights Act of 1964*. Minneapolis, MN: Abdo Publishing, 2016.

## Websites

To learn more about Presidential Perspectives, visit **booklinks.abdopublishing.com**. These links are routinely monitored and updated to provide the most current information available.

Visit **mycorelibrary.com** for free additional tools for teachers and students.

# INDEX

# ABOUT THE AUTHOR

Moira Rose Donohue practiced law for 20 years before becoming a children's book author. She has written many books for young people. She and her husband divide their time between northern Virginia and central Florida.